BE A BUSINESS GENERAL

**The secrets of teamwork in business, and why you
should lead your business from the front**

Frank Norving

Sommario

INTRODUCTION

Every business is founded with hopes of success.

Every startup today hopes to get to the very peak of its market segment and lay down the rules by which other companies are forced to pay.

Every entrepreneur dreams of the highest peaks of his industry.

It is the only thing that binds every entrepreneur. We may have different ideas, products, services, and opinions about how to get things done but the sure thing is that we all want to succeed at the things we do. We want to be the next hot thing on *Forbes* and get featured on the biggest business platforms as an example of success.

That is the expectation, but the stark reality couldn't be more different. The business world is a most treacherous environment. Against hopes, many people fail woefully at business. Despite their best intentions, many people never get a whiff of business successes.

Now, failure is a subjective term in business, but we can choose three spots at which most businesses fail. The first group of business failures occurs at inception. Perhaps due to weak ideas and bad plans, many businesses never seem to make it off the starting board. Problems may include a lack of capital, unfeasible ideas, inability to raise a team of employees willing to work and problems with the law.

The second group fails after the initial launch. They actually get started but never get to enjoy any success of note. This is where most businesses perish. A lack of unique ideas, weak marketing, poor service delivery, and bad business ethics stump businesses at this point and strangle them to death. Businesses can get trapped in ruts lasting years in this cycle. A little success is always followed by immediate losses. Most businesses that fail start to fail here.

The last type of failures is the most pathetic. They are the businesses that were once successful but slipped out of the success zone gradually and could not keep up with changing market demands and forces. Such companies may not fail at once, but still, a huge loss of market share represents a failure of some kind.

Are you an aspiring or existing entrepreneur? How can you ensure your business does not end up a failure? What steps can you take to give your business the best chance of surviving and thriving irrespective of how difficult the circumstances are? This is the focus of this book; to teach you how to be a success by leading from the frontline, because 95% of the time, that is the reason why businesses fail- a lack of good leadership.

You may have a great idea or limitless capital, but if you do not know how to lead your team, you are doomed for failure after failure. It does not matter that you have the greatest hands; if you do not give them the right directions and instructions, they will fail woefully. Therein lies the greatest risk to your endeavor to succeed in business.

Many businesses fail because the owner had an idea, sourced for capital, developed a great product, and then left anything else for the team he had assembled. You cannot afford to do this if you want to succeed. The greatest businessmen in history have always taken a hands-on approach that kept them in the loop at all time. This is what you must mirror too.

You have to build your personality up and then give that personality to your business. To succeed, you have to sit in the trench with your employees and direct the action from the frontline. It is the missing ingredient in business leadership classes that nobody ever tells you. This book is a practical guide for you to achieve the kind of success you want.

Good luck as I hope to help you build the business of your dreams.

CHAPTER ONE

SELF-BELIEF, THE STARTING POINT OF BUSINESS SUCCESS

"Always remember you are braver than you than you believe, stronger than you seem, and smarter than you think."

- Christopher Robin

Self-confidence and belief are the first ingredients in any endeavor in life.

You are going to meet too many obstacles to have any residue of uncertainty within you. Therefore, it is crystal clear that strong belief is responsible for a reasonable level of performance. If you desire to achieve anything great, the first thing you have to get along with your performance is a firm belief in your ability to actually pull your plans off.

Your belief drives your action, and your actions determine how far you can go.

When you a firm belief in yourself, your actions become better, smarter, and resilient with time. Self-belief applies and extends to all ramifications of life, which include athletics, business, personal relationship, education, and the likes. Belief is a two-way thing; your level of belief either gives you courage or places unsurmountable limitations on you.

Courageous belief boosts your performance, while the kind of belief that places a limitation on you reduces your performance. This can be very important when you are faced with a challenging situation, or you are under pressure. Fortunately, what you have belief in is your choice.

Win in Your Mind First

When you are under much pressure, it is impossible for you to rise to the occasion if you are not sufficiently confident.

If you have self-doubt, you are likely to sink back to a very low level. Being faced with a challenging situation places pressure on you mentally.

Your talent is not sufficient for you to address this; neither is physical training. How great a performance you are able to put in, shows how strong your belief is; people with great performance have the deepest and strongest belief. They have made a conscious effort to win in their minds first.

As a business leader, you have no hope of getting people to believe in your vision if you do not believe in yourself first.

The moment you give any sign of self-doubt, the people around you pick it up and make it impossible for you to get their full loyalty.

History is replete with examples of followers who followed their leaders blindly. Through fire, and through water, these followers went. All the times this happened, what do you think was the propelling force? The belief of course.

Let us take an example here.

Mohammed, the Moslem prophet, was once faced with an impossible scenario. He had fled Mecca, his hometown, due to persecution, to the town of Yathrib where he was welcomed. However, the Meccans soon marched on Yathrib determined to root out Mohammed and his band of followers. In those days, Mecca was the most important town in the Arabian Peninsula as the center of commerce and religion.

So, the Meccans were naturally well-equipped and had a large army of over one thousand men ready and trained for war.

In response, Mohammed and his followers only totaled three hundred and thirteen; most of them untrained for war and poorly equipped.

These two armies clashed at the plain of Badr, and the result of the war reshaped the Arabian Peninsula story. The Mohammed army fought with surprising aggressiveness and total determination and routed the Meccans who had to return home, tail between their legs.

What happened that hot afternoon has remained a lesson in confidence and leadership for future generations. Spurred by the unshakable confidence of their leader, the smaller army imbued self-belief that was simply stronger than the skills of the Meccans.

The presence of their leader and general on the field of war itself gave them further cause for courage as opposed to the Meccans who were fighting on instructions relayed from the back of the army. In the end, courage and belief won the smaller army a victory that nobody could have predicted.

The same thing happens in the business world all the time. Those who are able to get people to believe in them form an unshakable team that can overcome the prevailing market forces. This is almost always due in large part to the belief of the leader of the team.

Nobody is going to fight a battle to victory for you if they are not sure you expect a victory. Not in the business world anyway.

You cannot gain the full attention of the people around you, employees, or clients if you do not believe in what you are selling to them. It is the first law of making a sale.

Nobody wants to buy what you are selling if you do not believe in it.

Unless you have some other thing such as reputation going for you or a fantastic, unbeatable product, you won't sell anything without believing in the product and your ability to sell it. Self-belief is the staple of convincing other people.

Why is Belief So Powerful?

The powerful effect of strong belief lies in its ability to give you four things of great importance. Let us look at each of this.

- **Resilience**: This is the ability to make your way to the top after you must have undergone an adverse situation. It is the skill that holds you still while you are suffering setbacks, difficulties, and challenges. Strong belief serves as empowerment for people to become very resilient. It is responsible for backing up one's ability to respond to any situation with doggedness, determination, and tenacity. People with great performance place their confidence and focus on what needs to be done irrespective of the odds. Their time and energy are not wasted nagging, worrying, and making complaints. Much time is vested in the necessaries; they never quit, give in, or give up. If the situation seems harder, they tend to get better.

The logical thing when you face a hard situation is for you to turn back from it and try something else. That is precisely why logical people never succeed. Instead, resilience gives you the ability to forge a path through even the hardest of circumstances. Resilience is not a logical trait though. It goes against the grains of human nature. Therefore, the only way you can actually remain resolute in the face of hard circumstances is if you believe you have the ability to weather all storms and succeed. This is only one of the reasons why you must strive always to be confident.

- **Strong Willpower**: strong willpower can be said to be the effective alignment of perseverance, discipline, commitment, and consistency. This alignment is the drive that makes you better and keeps you motivated every minute of every day. Having a strong will goes beyond the commitment to get started, but rather the courage to move on against all the odds. When things get hard, belief is responsible for saying, "I will," and that may just be the spark that keeps you in the game.

- **Vision**: Strong belief is responsible for creating the vision; it gives you the foresight to see what is yet to be accomplished. Strong belief set the goals and understands the path you need to go through to achieve your goal. It makes for easy visualization of what has to be done, including training, practice, performance, and achievements. Once you have a vision, it is only belief that can guide you as you hone in towards your targets.

• **Activation of your potential**: A unique thing that belief does to the human body is the unleashing of your great potential. It is embedded with laser focus; it gets rid of distraction and doubts that can hinder your goal. It makes your efficiency reach the maximum capacity. Belief is going to trigger your skills and ability to make them work at their pace. When you are undergoing pressure, mostly competitive, the belief you have determines how far you will be able to utilize your capabilities to the fullest. So many people have worked hard to step up their ability, but in the long run, they are unable to gain full access to their capabilities due to distraction and negative thinking. Believing in yourself ignites the activation of your potential to prevent this;

only talent is not enough; you have to engage yourself mentally fully.

It is essential to note that belief should not be narrowed down to only individual performance. It can be a handy tool to facilitate team performance. A team united by one belief can be considered to be most excellent as their aim will be driven by real commitment and confidence. As your team leader though, the direction and level of self-belief you imbue your team is your sole prerogative. You need to ensure you keep your team motivated through self-belief and team belief.

CHAPTER TWO

BE AN ATTENTIVE LISTENER

"Of all the skills of leadership, listening is the most valuable – and one of the least understood. Most captains of industry listen only sometimes, and they remain ordinary leaders. But a few, the great ones, never stop listening. That's how they get word before anyone else of unseen problems and opportunities."   *- Peter Nulty*

To lead, you need to learn to be a great listener.

Verbal communication is the clearest form of communication within a team. I add chats and text messages to verbal communication for clarity sake. How your team-members communicate within the team, and with their target clients is down solely to you.

Most important however is your communication with your team. It is the medium by which you communicate your vision and give instructions. It is also doubly important the other way around.

You must also be alert to receive all tips and communication coming your way from your team.

Verbal communication is in different forms, which include listening and speaking.

In an ideal business setting, having listening skills is crucial to building a better relationship and create an enabling environment between the employees, management, and staff.

Also, it is essential to building better customer relationships. However, there are things you must do to be a good listener such as maintaining eye contact to show that your attention is totally for the person addressing you. Once the person is done speaking, rephrase his statement and ask him to confirm if you have gotten his point to be doubly sure. Ask reasonable questions until you have full knowledge of the messages being passed.

Attentive listening gives you the ample opportunity to garner facts so that you will be able to make a decision that will contribute to the growth of your business.

It is of the utmost importance when trying to build trust and reduce conflict rates.

Why should you listen attentively?

- **Gain Information**: It gives you the chance of discovering facts that are essential in making wise business decisions. For instance, this can be evident in an interview conducted for an applicant. You will get to know his ability and how he can handle the profession when employed.

More importantly, if you listen well enough, you will be able to discern the attitude of the applicant towards his previous jobs. All these will give you the insight to determine if the applicant is qualified to render good service for you. Again, an employer who is always willing to listen to any issue raised by the employee concerning their health will reduce injury and ensure better job performance. You cannot glean every fact from a piece of paper. Personal contact and attentive listening will give you a lot of hidden information and stimulate your instinct to take the right actions.

- **Develop and Build Trust**: When it comes to building trust in an organization, attentive listening is vital. A failure of a project might set in if any of the team members fails to listen and adhere by the instructions. In developing trust, ensure you pay maximum attention to the guidelines and deadlines stated. Take your time and listen to the remarks made by a worker or employee about his ability. We are all humans, and we all like our opinions to be regarded and respected at all times. Many business leaders fail this test. Do not dismiss anybody's ideas out of hand. Listen to them; it makes them feel like a part of the team even if their ideas are not accepted eventually. We all like to work better on tasks when we feel we have been a part of the decision-making process for the task. Utilize this loop to build trust in your team

- **Maintain Your Reputation**: Without mincing words, the reputation of your business also depends on your listening skills. Failure to attentively listen to a customer may probably lead to a customer not getting the product or kind of service she needs. If this occurs continuously, this will, in turn, tarnish the reputation of the company. On the other hand, if you exhibit good listening habits towards your clients and they are able to get the best of service from you, this will give you a good reputation. This translates directly into continued patronage and they can go as far as advertising your services to their friends and families. Let me cite a popular example here.

Nokia, the giant smartphone company, used to be at the top of the market chain at the start of the century. They made a lot of sales, especially in developing countries, and were respected for making, good quality, cheap mobile phones. Technology caught up as time went by, though; other companies started adding new features that excited their customers. Unfortunately, *Nokia* never listened to the market and the demands of their customers. They got left behind, and they have been playing catch-up ever since then. Today, they are no longer the force they once were; a lesson for all upcoming entrepreneurs.

- **Reduction in Conflict**: Conflicts are bound to arise in an organization; it occurs if any of the workers feels he's not treated right or misunderstood. A lot of mistakes, errors, and misconduct will not happen if all members of a team are on the same page.

Communication is essential to reduce these misunderstandings, and as the leader of the team, it is on you to ensure it is of the clearest, best quality possible.

- **Motivate Employees Through Listening**: The morale and the level of productivity of an employee can be heightened when the employer knows what serves as motivation for the employee. Taking note of the issues raised by workers to identify the particular aspect they are very good at or where they face challenges can spur them to develop even more creative solutions.

Knowing that the boss sounds interested in what you have found out can be the cue an employee needs to take more responsibility, assume leadership positions, and develop ingenious solutions far beyond his abilities.

The Difference Between Hearing and Listening

We hear through our ears, but listening happens through the mind. Both activities make use of the ear, but they are different things entirely. Hearing only helps you to receive sound waves and translate them into cogent data. On the other hand, listening takes this data and helps you put them in a logical form. With hearing, you pile up all the info you receive and mix them together in one loop of a jumble. In listening though, you are picking each thread of information and filing it away neatly in an appropriate place where you can retrieve it easily enough when you need it.

- Hearing can be considered as the ability of an individual to perceive sound, and this happens when you receive vibration through your ears. Listening is carried out with conscious effort and involves a detailed analysis and processing of the sounds received.
- Hearing can be considered as been physiological as it merely occurs making use of any of our sense organ. On the other hand, listening is a psychological act, i.e., with conscious effort

- Hearing is passive, while listening is active as your brain tries to fix meanings and draw trends from what is being heard.
- Hearing can be considered innate, while listening is sometimes a learned and acquired skill. Everybody hears but only a few people listen.

Listening is an advanced form of hearing. It goes beyond hearing words alone; it transcends the physical aspect of hearing. It is the conscious decision to understand somebody else's ideas, thoughts, moods, and hopes. It needs you to be mindful, and it brings home bountiful positive results.

CHAPTER THREE

RISING ABOVE BUSINESS FAILURE

"Failure is success if we learn from it."

— Malcolm Forbes

In business, you are bound to face some challenges. The ability to scale through the ups and down is what makes a successful entrepreneur stand out.

Being confronted by failure is inevitable; it can come in a variety of forms, big or small.

It will probably be a huge disappointment when it happens; losing a big deal or contract to your competitor or having difficulty clearing your payroll, for instance. However, an outstanding entrepreneur is not always defined by failures and loss they have suffered during the cause of their business.

Getting to maneuver your way when faced with challenges, internal or external, is essential if you want to be successful in your business line.

However, there are ways in which you can better handle the situation, in such a way that it will serve as a stepping stone for you to attain a better height in your business

- **Get Prepared**: It may probably seem impossible for you to make absolute provision for contingency, but then having the mental preparedness and confidence to tackle failure is of utmost importance. Get ready to experience one or two setbacks. Every business does, and you will too. Do not beat yourself up or go on a destructive streak when you take a loss. Just take inventory, conduct a conscientious inquest, and get back out there. In short, getting yourself prepared is key to rising above business failures.

- **Know what invigorates you**: Having a better understanding of what you are about to do is very important. People that have insight about what they have to do always have clear thinking and have the necessary ability to face and overcome hardship. Above all, you should know the things that can refill your motivation tank whenever you are running low. Examples include exercise, spending time with loved ones, or isolating yourself to get inspiration.

• **Do not make an emotional decision:** People often make hasty decisions after facing something negative or disheartening. Decisions made in a rage or fit of anger or sadness, are always detrimental to our business life; those decisions can ruin the business. If you have just suffered a loss or disappointment during the cause of business, ensure you take at least five minutes to break just for you to clear your head. When you make decisions that are rational over the emotional choices, you are making a step further towards resolving the complicated issue.

• **Build a strong support network:** Ensure you surround yourself with people who are of a positive mind that genuinely have an interest in seeing you succeed. They will make you feel loved and tend to be very supportive while you go through your hard times. They are also likely to give you honest advice that may help you get a better grasp of the situation.

- **Reevaluate your situation:** The best thing you have to do to pick up the pieces after you must have failed is to reevaluate yourself. Find out the reason why you failed, how you felt after failing, and the action you should take next. If the rate of productivity in your company dropped drastically, this is just an opportunity for you to have a rethink and figure out what has gone wrong. Could it be because you failed to do certain things? Are your employees in a rut? At times failure passes the message that what you are engaging yourself in is not intended for you. The moment you can figure out this, and honestly advise yourself, you will be able to save your time, energy, become happy, and live a purposeful life. Forget the wasted efforts of the past, and evaluate the current situation to help you make better decisions for the future.

- **Do not be too serious with yourself**: Try to avoid self-pity; failure is inevitable in life. Some may make you think that it is the end of the world, but having a strong belief that everything is going to be alright in the end is key. The failures are there to either instruct you or teach you new things. Do not make them a rod for your own back.

- **Do not identify with failure as a person**: It is normal that when things go bad, the team leader blames himself for the problems. Yes, you should always take responsibility but in a constructive form. All humans have to deal with failure at one point in their life. Just imagine what the world is going to look like if everybody gets what they want quickly. Attaching yourself firmly to failure will make things get worse, and it will be difficult to resolve. Do not consider yourself a perennial failure. Just work towards your next goal and plan instead.

- **Do not dwell on failure**: If we are to look at history, failure seems to be a background story for all successful people. J.K. Rowling was a divorced, poor mother of one when she wrote the Harry Potter stories. Getting a publisher to like the book was just as hard. Today, we are all in awe of her writing skills. Steve Jobs was thrown out of his own company. Walt Disney was fired by his editor for not being creative enough. Do you know how they got beyond their failure? They went past their failure by walking past it and leaving it firmly in the past. The editor that sacked Disney, the publishers that rejected Harry Potter and the executives that got Jobs out of *Apple,* were all left in the past by the people concerned, and that represented the ultimate in productive response to criticism. Do not allow your past to hold you down; use it as a springboard and motivation for the future.

- **Learn from the past**: Insanity is said to be doing the same thing the same way and expecting a different result. I have not asked you to throw away your past and shut it out. Instead, learn from it, process the sequence of decision that led to failure, pick the lessons, and then discard the negative emotions. You have to make sure you know why you failed and avoid anything that can lead to a repeat of that mistake.

- **Have a proper understanding of what you are engaging yourself in**: Being an entrepreneur, you are competing against a lot of forces. The best thing you can do before you venture into business or branch out into new areas is to conduct a proper analysis of what you are about to get into. Understand the factors for and against you, and plan ahead for them. That way, you know when things are going south, and you can adjust accordingly.

CHAPTER FOUR

STAY SHARP AND ASK QUESTIONS

"Creativity flows when curiosity is stoked."

– Neil Blumenthal

I always mention in my books that you cannot do the same thing everyone is doing, in the same way, and hope to succeed more than most people.

The only way to stand out is to stay creative. Curiosity is a currency for success. You need to stay sharp to identify opportunities for your business to thrive. It is a short path to success. It is easier to broach new areas than attempt to take over an existing market using the same strategies everyone around you is doing.

You need to promote an atmosphere of curiosity in the frontlines for your business.

Intellect and expertise are now held responsible for delivering solutions to all questions and problems that clients might have.

In some organizations, employees are not allowed to say they don't outrightly know something. The higher you go on the corporate ladder, the lesser the tolerance level for not understanding anything at all. Do not allow the creative sand run out of your business; encourage brainstorming at all levels. In fact, make it a point to ensure that employees know that you respect, reward, and appreciate curiosity and ingenuous solutions to problems.

The term curiosity on its own can be said to be the operating system that gives room for the creation of something new.

As an entrepreneur and leader, the ability to create, explore, think, market, and innovate will determine how efficient your work will be. One of the gurus in management, Peter Drucker, is popular with his classification of the two functions of business which include marketing and innovation.

The success of your business is solely dependent on how well you can innovate new services, products, system, and processes. This will improve the quality of goods and services delivered to your customers so that you can stand out among peers.

When you look at a process like everyone else, you are merely a passive observer. The moment you show high curiosity, you automatically become an active observer immediately. You become someone capable of triggering a breakthrough. It doesn't matter if you do not discover anything new. Being curious alone has its own rewards. If nothing else, you gain a better understanding of the business process. That knowledge can come in pretty handy in the near future.

Curiosity is the reason technology continues to move the human race forward at supersonic speed. A millennium ago. Humans were intrigued by how birds could fly in the sky. Nobody knew how they did it; yet, treatises and theories were propounded from the genuinely absurd to spiritual explanations. It felt impossible for us to fly through the air at that time, but humans never stopped wondering and trying.

Millions of attempts later, the Wilbur brothers finally achieved the impossible; humans could begin to fly. That is an example of what base, primal curiosity can deliver. By asking questions, we learned to ask the right questions. By learning to ask the right questions, we got the first answers. It didn't matter that they were wrong. They led us to the right answer. With the right answers, we got the right solution. We would not be flying through the sky at speeds faster than birds if we didn't ask questions in the beginning.

Learning through curiosity

Of course, it is crystal clear that interest increases our knowledge. It is almost impossible for us to learn something and know very much about it at the same moment.

How deep we get to learn about new things is solely dependent on how much we open our minds, leaving aside what we think we know and getting to learn some new ideas.

In short, curiosity is a lens that allows you to see things in an entirely new dimension, irrespective of your level of experience. For you to be a leader with genuine curiosity, it is of utmost importance for you to suspend your knowledge, skills, and assumptions while you attempt to learn new things. You must be objective and direct your mental and emotional consciousness to ask constructive questions and see results as being open-ended.

The moment you get ourselves into this state of

mind, you are now open to the world of possibilities.

The moment you become a curious person, you will begin to ask the right questions and find the right answers.

Tools for cultivating curiosity

Having expressly stated that curiosity fuels creative solutions and theorized its benefits in our life and business, here are the two tools for achieving that heightened level of sensitivity.

- Asking a lot of questions is the way forward. Consider childhood. The natural curiosity we are all born with led us to ask many questions, some outright awkward and offensive. Asking those questions though taught us a lot of things. The same thing applies even now. Ask questions, and you will get answers. Look critically at processes and market needs. Read and conduct a lot of mini-researches to test your theories, and you will soon have answers that others still seek.
- Try to listen without judgment. Most times, we make a quick assumption about people when we listen to them; this is not a very good trait. That will impede your bid to

apply the principles of curiosity. Curious people love to have a clear sight of other people's perspectives. They absorb info without prejudice and then process it to find the answers they seek. Do not allow bias to block your curiosity gene.

The Business Value of Curiosity

Attaining success in business involves you putting conscious efforts in so many things which includes creativity, courage, and skills, among others. Put together, the importance of curiosity in business includes;

- Building a better customer relationship. It is just natural in people to be attracted to those who are interested in their affairs. You tend to know new things about people and make deeper connections when you have an abiding fascination. This can also go well in negotiating and winning contracts. The personal touch also allows you to customize your preferences to their taste.

- Increases your business acumen; when you are curious about tour business, you will be motivated to learn new things. In the process of learning new things, there is reasonable improvement in your ability to offer the best services to your customers

- It is a fact that customers are always happy when solutions are provided to their problems. The only way you can get to offer a reasonable settlement is when you are driven by genuine curiosity about the state of things

- Instrumental in correcting sales errors. Curiosity teaches you to always inspect all processes; that could be a factor in determining new trends in business volume. If you suddenly lost or gained a lot of customers, curiosity teaches you to know the source of the upheaval. That will allow you to fix any leak or potential source of problem long before it becomes a large problem.

- It is also a driving force that leads to the creation of great products made with sophisticated and advanced technology to satisfy the needs of the customers

- Lastly, curiosity can go a long way in motivating your employees. Bonding together to proffer new solutions can double the productive potential of a team. By infusing curiosity into the business ethic of your setup, you guarantee a constant stream of brilliant idea and creative suggestions.

Curiosity is the soul of creativity; it gives you the right ideas and the right questions to ask. Therefore, you must always be ready to ask questions and also learn new things every minute of the day.

Make yourself a bastion of information; create a system that actually works within your business. Teach your employees to stay alert and open to any new information that concerns your business. It is your work as a leader if you want to be successful.

CHAPTER FIVE

WHY YOU SHOULD PAY ATTENTION TO ALL DETAILS

"The universe is full of noise. True wisdom knows what to pay attention to."

– Debasish Mridha

Paying attention to details is very important in business; it helps in preventing mistakes and gives way for success to happen. In every business, there are some essential element that makes up the business. It ranges from the tangible to intangible things, physical and non-physical.

If a company does not have a leader that pays attention to all the details, many things will go wrong.

The non-tangible aspect that should be catered for which include the quality of the service rendered, the efficacy of the products, and the reliability of the support service. However, it is of utmost importance to know the difference between good and great.

The difference is 'if' and 'how' you pay attention to the key factors which include the visible and invisible ones.

In most cases, the companies that go bankrupt and the business that fail do so because they refused to pay attention to the necessary details. On the other hand, most businesses that work out well have taken due cognizance of every action and possible reactions. For instance, we are in a world where everything changes from time to time.

You may have a product of high quality that you want to offer to people, but if you are not conscious of the market forces at work, you will find little to no sales.

It is understandable that in business, many issues arise at once that need to be addressed within a short timeframe. That creates a scale of preference, and you will prioritize some over others. It looks like a brilliant and convenient solution, but the real issue is that every single detail has the potential to count in a big way if not taken care of.

Therefore, it is important to learn efficiency at work; to create more time to deal with more details, and also delegate under thorough supervision. Some techniques for this include;

- Get yourself organized. This is not to say you should always tidy up your stuff, or waste your precious time going through some kinds of stuff. You can get yourself organized by making use of the calendar. Just ensure you mark out the necessary plans, appointments, and meetings. That way, you know exactly how much work you can take in a day. Additionally, it means you know exactly what you should be doing at every point in time.

- Making a list is also crucial. Some people think a regimented list hinders creativity. In the real sense, though, it boosts your creativity as it saves you the stress related to multitasking and allows you to set your priorities right. A to-do list offers benefits revolving around organization and increased time management.

- Conscious limitation of distraction also goes a long way in creating more time. Getting distracted is inevitable; we encounter this almost everywhere, including at work. Get rid of the distractions that seem to take up far too much time out of your day.
- Try to embrace your routine. Having no routine can make you look undisciplined. Routines are always beneficial. it forces you to do some things continuously, and this teaches you to pay attention to the necessary details.

The Importance of Paying attention to Details

Paying attention helps you a lot in monitoring your business.

Have you ordered food to be delivered to you only to receive a poorly-packaged delivery? Or a late delivery? This kind of things discourage customers that may probably wish to patronize you in the future. As a business leader, all these things should be taken care of because if your clients observe a drop in quality, the patronage is going to drop.

Unfortunately, if you are not on your toes, a lot

of these things will happen. When you pay attention to the necessary details, you tend to build your credibility to some reasonable extent. This will make customers have confidence in your business.

Virtually all businesses are built on trust, and business propagation is built on trustworthiness. Paying attention also has benefits from a security point of view. It prevents you from being susceptible to fraud. There will always be a "smart-finger" employee looking to rip the business off. When you are firmly in the saddle though, the chances are you will spot such frauds quicker as you have access to all information. If opportunistic employees discover that you do not pay proper attention to certain details, they will consider that a loophole to defraud you and the business of its equity.

CHAPTER SIX

SUCCESS AS THE KEY FOR SUSTENANCE

"Successful people do what unsuccessful people are not willing to do. Don't wish it were easier; wish you were better."

– Ray Goforth

Many business leaders achieve success in the course of their business, yet only a few of them have the ability to sustain this initial success for a very long time.

Ensuring steady growth of business requires you to have the proper intellectual capital, and create a strategic partnership between you and your employees, and you and your clients. Aside from this, your business has to be based around a service whose market demand is high.

Aside from the above-listed fundamentals; you

will need a strong operational foundation, one that ensures you can take calculated risks that will sustain the growth of your business.

As an example, let's assume that you have been running an IT-based company that offers quality service and consultancy. Perhaps, you are quite sure that if you expand, you can generate revenues five times as large as what you currently pull in. To help things better, you just created a new service that seems to be in high demand. What do you do? Most people would do one of two extremes; one, they may develop cold feet at the prospect of suddenly becoming five times as big a company as they were. The other group of people would jump at that opportunity so hard that they would leap before looking, and land in hot water.

Instead, a smart businessman would consider the Pros and Cons; variables such as the absence of top talent, inadequate operational efficiencies, and poor service delivery will need to be fixed as you do not want them to drag you back. To address this, you need to create a productive environment that will strengthen your employees, get the right team together, form an external relationship with associates, and then make a strategic decision. Before you can sustain the growth of your business, you must consider taking action on some of the points listed below.

- Top Talent: If the right people are absent in your team, you will not have sustainable growth over time. As a leader, you should know that business is all about people, and without having the right people with you, there can't be sustainable growth and development. Most times, it is always at the best interest of a leader to refresh the talents of its employees to meet the needs of your clients for continuous patronage. Also, jolt existing members by sending them on extra competence drives.

- Operational Efficiency: In short, having efficiency in the organization minimizes the cost of operation and allows for cooperation within your team. This helps to give assurance that the mode of operation of a business has relevance for sustainable growth. In creating operational efficiency, be very confident that you create a workplace culture that drives efficiency within the organization

- Prospecting for the Right Clients: In this modern world, you cannot narrow down entrepreneurship to a typical business term.

Instead, it can be considered as a way of life. It is of utmost importance for you to embrace the right attitude of an entrepreneur when it comes to making maximum use of any opportunity that comes your way. Understand your market; know the people you want to sell your product or service to, and sell to them in the best places possible.

• Sound Decision Making: As a leader, part of the work you are expected to do is to provide a lasting solution to problems that might occur in the business. This means that you must be able to tackle problems and not give up on delivering sustainable growth while you do that. If you put in a standard in place to run its affairs effectively, it will be easy to deal with the problem and make the right decision.

It seems very hard to create sustainable growth in a business environment where people are always being reactive, rather than be proactive. For you to make a sound decision, there must be good judgment and the ability to make the right timing to give the assurance of a strong momentum

- Great Leadership: In the business world, the ones with great success are always the ones that follow their instinct while making decisions, thereby giving them the circular vision to utilize the opportunity that comes their way effectively. The leadership needed in sustaining business growth is the one that can see a glass as half full, while everyone else sees it as being half-empty. That is why you are reading this book to become an even better leader

- Do Not Be Afraid to Grow: To have sustainable growth in your business, you must not be afraid of taking risks. The only thing that is required of you is to make sure you take a calculated risk. If employees notice fear in you, they will not be motivated to share their ideas with you. It becomes much more challenging to take charge of the needs of the business, which in turn makes the market place to start passing you by. The sustenance of your business success requires you to relate and share your momentum with all members of the team. It's not something that can be done singlehandedly. You need to carry others along actively to make way for the right-thinking intellectual capital. The moment sustainability becomes a significant part of your organization. Then you will not be able to sustain only growth but also stay several steps ahead of your competitors.

CHAPTER SEVEN

BE UNIQUE AND ALLOW YOUR BUSINESS TO BE UNIQUE

A brand for a company is like a reputation for a person. You earn reputation by trying to do hard things well.

– Jeff Bezos

There are over ten thousand different species of birds in the world. These birds are of various sizes, different shapes, and they possess different abilities. Of these different species, there is one that stands out the most. This species is not the biggest neither is it the smallest; what sets this specie apart is how unique it is. I am talking about the eagle.

The eagle is the emblem of many countries and different organizations because of its distinctive characteristics. The eagle is known for its extraordinary vision, great strength, good looks, and longevity. It must be said that no bird in the universe has a combination of these unique traits; hence, none stands out as the eagle. The eagle has a lot to teach business owners, or will it suffice to say that business owners have a lot to learn from the "king of the birds."

The business world today is filled with inventors and creators who believe that "good artists copy, and great artist steal." Consequently, lots of businesses are replicates and duplicates of different ideas. Hence, products or services look like boring clones, lacking any sort of stand-out features.

Dear reader, the aim of this chapter is not to discourage the act of being inspired by the ideas of others. The aim is to ensure that uniqueness becomes a distinctive feature of whatever you plan to do. It must be stated that what you do as a business, the problem you solve as a company and the need your product satisfies does not matter if it is not done uniquely. In other words, it is not what you do; it is how you do it.

A few years ago, nobody was expecting a new taxi company to become highly successful, because the streets were already filled with different taxis sharing the same passengers. If anything, it was looking like a saturated business niche. That was until the emergence of the taxi-hailing service *Uber*, which came into the market with its unique offering - safer taxis at the push of a button.

Today, the company is the largest taxi company in the world; interestingly, they do not own a single taxi. Now, that was a unique idea!

Hotels, motels, guest houses, and apartments were the only form of guest accommodation available for a long time. Did they provide accommodation to hordes of tourists, visitors, and lovers of the hospitality business?

Yes, they did.

But when *Airbnb* came into the scene, they offered a completely different idea, one that the rest of the field could not compete with.

They delivered to their teeming customer's the same quality of accommodation that is obtainable in big hotels but at a very affordable rate. Interestingly, feedback from guests suggested that they feel more at home in an Airbnb than in a hotel. Now, that was unique!

When airplanes were invented, it represented a leap for the entire human race.

People, goods, and services could easily be transported over boundaries and across long distance in record time. The mere fact that we were flying in the sky seemed to be a peak on its own. However, on the 2nd of March 1969, the world was stunned when the Concorde jet made its first flight as the fastest plane in the world.

You might ask what made the Concorde unique? Well, the designers of the Concorde jet made a fast means of transportation "faster." By introducing a new dimension into their market, the ensured they were the only company anyone that needed a truly fast plane would come to. Now, that was unique!

You can call them disruptors, you can call them iconoclasts, you can even call them anarchists, but the reason you are talking about these businesses, these companies, and their unique products is BECAUSE their ideas stood out when other businesses couldn't. Let us take one more example.

How did a tiny music player become a technological

and popular product? Listen to the story of *Apple*'s iPod. *Sony Corporation* might have kick-started the portable music player revolution, but it was *Apple* led by Steve Jobs that truly got it up and running. The Walkman, a music player made by *Sony,* was large, clumsy and not aesthetically appealing to the younger generation. This is what the iPod came to change. The iPod was not just beautiful aesthetically, it could store lots of music and in the words of Steve Jobs, "you can put your entire music collection in your pocket." The mere impact of that idea gave the iPod wings to soar above its competitors and become a commercial marvel.

There is only one way to stand out in business just as we have learned from the eagle and other successful companies; don't blend in, don't give in, just stand out! Allow your uniqueness to speak for you.

Allow your name to speak for you

Apple, Amazon, Coca Cola, Google, Nike, Microsoft, Mercedes Benz, Samsung, and *Toyota* represent a list of commercial behemoths in the modern world. With revenues running into billions and billions of customers among them, these companies all play on their name to push forward new products.

Amongst all these companies though, none has the global appeal and reputation that *Coca-Cola* has. You might not know, but there is more to this company with a trademark red color and its sweet-tasting beverage. There are places in the world where you will not get clean water, but you will find a bottle of *Coca-Cola*.

The *Coca-Cola* success story is a lesson every company, every business, and every potential entrepreneur should learn, adapt and master in order to create a brand that sets them apart from their competition and attracts more customers. A lot of people do not know the story of a business that was founded as a drug company in the 19th century by John Pemberton. How did *Coca-Cola* become the world's premier global brand? What did *Coca-Cola* do to become the leading soda pop brand that is currently consumed by almost half of the world's population on a regular basis?

Coca-Cola built a name for themselves by developing an unduplicatable recipe which made them stand out from their closet competition. Just like every company with a unique product, *Coca-Cola's* recipe was good but not good enough to make them the number one beverage brand in the world immediately. *Coca-Cola* combined the dual strength of "great product and great marketing" to capture the attention of the world and to cement the name of its product in the heart of every consumer out there.

Not only was the product addictive, but it was also fast selling, and as record sales began to climb, a lot of competitors sought to tap into the growing market. What did *Coca-Cola* do to maintain its grasp upon its niche? The company invested millions of dollars in celebrity-endorsed advertorials and record-breaking yet controversial advertorials like the Thanda Matlab television advertorial campaign in India which introduced the brand to the Indian market. By leveraging on the uniqueness of the product, the marketability of celebrity ambassadors and the reputation of *Coca-Cola*, the legend that *Coca-Cola* is today, was born and cemented.

You need to know that businesses only thrive when the names of the brand speak for the brand. When it comes to mobile phones, most Americans go for *Apple* because the brand *Apple* speaks for itself. The name on the lips of most online shoppers when they need swift, safe and reliable online purchases is *Amazon*. The list is endless. This is the secret of *McDonalds*, *Starbucks,* and other mega brands. It makes it easier for them to push new rules and products (even those that do not match up to expectations). It becomes easier for them to get away with little infractions and drops in quality. Of course, this does not last for too long, or it would become noticeable.

It was an almost impossible task to turn a drug into a drink. It was hard to compete with other established brands. It was hard to convert a company that only sold a few drinks in its first year to a business that counts its customers in billions. That is the point. You will get rewarded for staying unique all the time. If not in sales, then in reputation.

All it took *Coca-Cola* was a few strategies but most importantly, consistency and a unique and fresh approach. The good thing about uniqueness is that it never ends. Tomorrow, a company might rise to modify *Coca-Cola*'s approach even further and introduce a twist into that industry. Uniqueness never stops.

There is always a market for you

Billions of birds fly in the sky each day. It doesn't even matter if they all fly at once; the sky is large enough to take them all. The message in this is that if your idea is good enough, the market will expand to give you a share. If there is no space for expansion, then the market will contract to squeeze out redundant ideas and hand over their clients to you. It happened in the Smartphone industry a few years ago. True global giants like *Nokia* and *RIM* (developers of the Blackberry line of phones) lost their clients as punishment for not keeping up with market trends.

Upcoming business owners are often paralyzed at the sight of other competing ideas. Scared of the hardships involved in breaking into already established monopolies, many ideas die a natural death occasioned by fear. The solution to this is to understand that it is possible to birth a unique product or start a unique business if you understand market segments.

Coca-Cola had already captured a large chunk of the market before their closest and eternal rivals, Pepsico came into the market. For many, the presence of *Coca-Cola* was a signal that that particular niche held no prospects for new players, but *PepsiCo* understood that it was possible to fly in the "beverage sky" without running into or being run over by *Coca-Cola*.

Today, *PepsiCo* is a giant in its own right, makes a large profit, and has about 22 different brands underneath her umbrella. Just when the world thought that *PepsiCo* had finally sealed the effective duopoly of that industry, a Canadian company, *Virgin Drinks* was set up to capture the percentage of market share left. Not only did *Virgin Cola* become a serious force in the pop soda industry, it even started to rival the big two – *Coca-Cola* and *Pepsi*.

The lesson for you in this story is that there is always a space for you in every segment if you have a unique product or a new approach to marketing or delivery of service.

Brands like *Forever 21*, *Michael Kors* and *Philip Plein* have a message for you; "There is always a market for you." This group of companies was fashion newbies who came into the highly competitive fashion business when the market was already dominated and being ruled by behemoths like *Nike*, *Adidas*, *Armani*, *Gucci* and *D &G* brands. Not only did these new upstarts survive, but they also thrive today.

The story of *Amazon*, which began as an online book store, and today has become the largest online store is equally inspiring for entrepreneurs. *Amazon* went for 70 percent of an untapped market. It was at the beginning of the technology boom; Silicon Valley was crawling with technological whiz kids who were either inventing a new device or creating the trendiest app. Jeff Bezos could have joined this herd of inventors and created 'just another app,' which he could sell off for a couple of million; instead, he chose a path less traveled. He chose e-commerce and the results astounded even Bezos.

Setting up an online book store was cool then but it wasn't the rave of the moment. *eBay* and *Craigslist* represented the major competition the new company was going to have, but Jeff's ideas of delivery were much different from others. So began Amazon's began a journey of dominance that has led Jeff Bezos to the top of the world's rich list. Amazon reached the zenith of the e-commerce market in less than three decades because it focused on the untapped and unexplored 70 percent of the market. It was not about the uniqueness of the idea for this company. Rather, it was the uniqueness of its market section that brought success.

As the source of ideas for your own business, focus on creating unique products and services. If you do not have this, then create a new way of service delivery. If all this fail, then spot a market that nobody knows existed as Amazon did. Whatever you do, just make sure it stands out clearly. Let it become your identity and the market forces will reward you for throwing up a new idea. The market always does. Ask *Coca-Cola* if you doubt me.

CHAPTER EIGHT

YOUR TEAM AND GRATITUDE

"Gratitude is a recognition of our interdependence, of the fact that success is the result of team effort."

–*Naz Beheshti*

For a long time, the work environment has been an environment notable for celebrating the strong, encouraging competition, and appreciating only the exceptional individual or act. While this resulted in outstanding results, speedy task delivery, and a passion for excellence, the workplace sadly lost more than it gained by adopting this approach.

The workplace lost the spirit of interdependence;

the workplace lost the feeling of camaraderie; it traded valuable relationships for a quasi-transactional relationship.

Staff members became used to associating pay rise or perks as the company's response to excellent work and compliments were rarely used except when the management was in "high spirit," while condemnation became the order of the day.

On the outside, most companies looked well, on the inside, everything was wrong. Only the top performers among employees seem to get extra appreciation; the others only got their paychecks at the end.

The initial idea was that perks might promote competitiveness, but that isn't quite right. The truth is that there will always be top performers and average performers. When all the appreciation is reserved for those at the top, the remaining members of the staff quickly learn their places.

They realize that they cannot compete for the extra gratitude; so, they settle for what they are doing now. Unmotivated, unhappy they cannot compete, standards of work and productivity begins to drop. That is why a lot of companies go under or return reduced revenue.

In a typical small business today, the books might look good, and the workforce might feign comfort and job satisfaction to the outside world, but if a keen observer pays enough attention, you might discover that things are gradually falling apart because gratitude which is meant to be at the center of the corporate culture doesn't hold. It is possible for the manager, and the managed, the leader and the led, the boss and the subordinates to limit the workplace to a place meant for work and no warmth. This is counterproductive though.

A study on the effect of gratitude was conducted a few years ago, and the results were very astonishing. Nine out of ten employees claimed to be motivated, inspired, and psyched to give in more time and energy whenever their bosses showed appreciation or when their colleagues noticed them or their efforts. This figure represents a startling ninety percent of the staff of a company with over 1000 staff members. The other 10 percent claimed to be indifferent to compliments.

The result of this survey exposed a vital truth that most workplaces fail to realize, no matter the output of a business or a staff, staffs are humans, not machines.

Machines do not need encouragement; neither do

they respond to criticism.

Machines do not face tough economic situations or battle with addictions; only humans do.

Great companies have discovered this secret, the secret of encouraging results and effectively complimenting and celebrating these efforts that led to these results.

With this, they are able to raise effective teams that feel appreciated and motivated. Great managers or great managements have realized that the feeling of efficiency is proportional to the feeling a staff has when they feel valued by their bosses and colleagues.

When a team-member is appreciated, they feel competent about the work they do, and they feel confident that their place in the business is secure. When this becomes a corporate culture, the feeling of wellness spreads in the workplace.

A lot of people erroneously assume that being grateful is a sign of weakness, especially if it comes from a boss or the leader of a team. Being grateful is not being vulnerable. After all, both the leader and the led are humans, and success is a product of a combined effort. Influential leaders know that success is a product of communal effort, and they also know that interdependence is the foundation of every healthy and wealthy team.

Why you need to appreciate your team-members

It was Maya Angelou who said, "People will forget what you said to them, but they will not forget how you made them feel." We all know how we feel when we are appreciated. We also know how we feel when we are under-appreciated or castigated. Sadly, it appears that not all leaders know this.

You must know that a workplace without happy team-members is a mere workstation no matter how beautiful it looks. Sadly, most leaders treat their businesses as work stations; they expect employees to come in, do a job mechanically, and get paid. Yes, that is the basic idea, but the better you make those employees feel, the better the work they will produce for you.

A lot of leaders spend time condemning their staff instead of commending them. Many business owners will rather make speeches praising themselves (or favorite team-members) rather than praising the entire team for working well to produce a result.

Newsflash! The reason why most employees are unhappy, morale is low, and tasks seem to be delayed is because employees have lost their motivation.

There are many more reasons why you should show every member of your team gratitude. Gratitude,

- Improves their productivity: Gratitude always results in improved productivity.

  The primary reason why most individuals underperform at their jobs is that they feel underappreciated or not appreciated at all. When individuals feel genuinely cared for because of the actions or words of gratitude from their colleagues and their superiors, they want to do more, and they always do more.

- Improves Team relationships: when people feel appreciated at work, they tend to become friendly with their staff and their bosses. As we all know, a friendly environment is a happy environment, and a happy environment is a great place to work.

It is possible to make a case for reduced productivity resulting from familiarity in a friendly work environment. While cases like this have been observed, the rewards of a workplace where there is high level of camaraderie outweighs the risk.

Gratitude encourages interdepartmental relationships, intradepartmental relationships, customer-company relationship, and other kinds of business relationships that can take your business higher.

- Improves general well-being and emotional balance: Studies show that gratitude is often linked with the release of dopamine (a feel-good hormone). Research haa also shown that the absence of this hormone or the presence of the hormone in minute quantities is linked to depression and several stress-related diseases. The healthier your team is, the fewer the sick days they need to take off. The happier your employees feel, the more optimistic they are to work. Wise leaders understand that being grateful is cheaper than being ungrateful, which is why they never miss an opportunity always, to do the former.

- Improves staff loyalty: think about this! A dog always hangs around the person that cares for it the most. Then, it should be no surprise that companies that show more gratitude to individual employees get to guarantee employees' loyalty better. Aside from the lure of more money and control, there is a fundamental logic behind why people leave their jobs in companies because they feel unappreciated, uncared for, and unnoticed. Even if the potential wage of a new employer seems better, it's been observed that most staff are not always motivated to leave jobs where they feel like a family. As a great leader, it is vital to know that the best way to keep staff is not by token gestures or pay increase. The most tested and trusted method is by deploying real, sincere and heartfelt gratitude.

Transactional Gratitude: the mistake leaders make

Before this chapter is concluded, it is critical to chip in this piece of information. In a bid to apply the principles of gratitude, most leaders fall into the trap of making gratitude more of a transactional act. They make gratitude an occasional act where empty words are used, and token gestures are employed.

Interestingly, team-members can always see through the veneer of such falsity and artificiality.

Transactional gratitude is reducing gratitude to a company program which occurs annually, weekly, or every first hour of the day. Some companies make gratitude seem like a sort of obligation, and consequently, they take away the essence behind such an incredible act.

Gratitude is not appreciation. Appreciation is a response to good work; appreciation is the company or the business rewarding an employee for loyalty after a long time, but gratitude is communicating through words and deeds how valuable a team member or staff is to you or the organization.

In conclusion, gratitude is not a "fake it till you make it" act. You need to be genuinely happy with your team-members for it to count.

CHAPTER NINE

THE POWERFUL EFFECT OF TEAMWORK

"Individual commitment to a group effort – that is what makes teamwork, a company work, a society work, a civilization work."

– Vince Lombardi

Humans are here as the dominant species on Earth because we have learned to work as a team better than any other species. Favored by nature to build social networks, we have transformed teamwork into a means of survival. Rules and societal morals keep us committed to this teamwork.

We perform better as a group than as individuals. Therefore, teamwork brings out the best in us. A team is a collection of two or more people united in purpose and plans to carry out an activity. Teamwork is particular to a group of people intending to work with maximum efficiency and collectively to achieve greater success. In the business world, the secret that binds the successful growth and development of a business is how efficient the team works.

For you to be an efficient team member, you have to have the ability and capability to function well as an individual. More importantly, it is for you to contribute reasonably when working collectively with other team members. For there to be a total accomplishment of the goals set, teamwork is essential. The requirement to be considered being a team member is simply a clear understanding of the goals and objectives such that the efforts made by individuals will be in correlation to the effort of the team.

As a leader and business entrepreneur, the secret is in knowing how to create teams to drive your ideas towards completion.

Benefits of Teamwork

As earlier stated, teamwork brings so many people together to ensure the maximum efficiency of the business process. There are different ways in which you can organize the team. Some are particularly designed for a particular product, while some are specially made for a process which includes research and manufacturing. Teamwork gives its members ample opportunity to gain more experience, promote morale, and engender innovation. Succinctly, teamwork gives room for innovation and creativity; it energizes individuals and provides the morale to work. Other benefits of teamwork will be subsequently discussed below.

- **Teamwork improves morale and promotes a sense of ownership and belonging**

Yes, I know it is your idea and business, but teamwork makes employees see themselves as the real owners of the business. They tend to work with all resources they can, given the fact that they see themselves as being in control of certain aspects of the business process. This will bring about a great improvement in morale. The extra effort put in by the team leads to a pleasant atmosphere for working. Every employee involved in teamwork always experiences a sense of belonging which in turn makes them proud of their work and team members. That can lay the foundation for increased productivity.

- **It builds trust and enhances the relationship**

Teamwork can help promote a better working relationship between the employer and his employees; each person learns how to disagree to agree and later come up with a good result. It creates an environment where the members of your team learn to win and lose together, celebrate and fix problems together, and genuinely appreciate the effort of every member of the team. It is possible for you as the leader to sit somewhere and share out tasks that compartmentalize the skills of individual employees, but such a model breeds loners incapable of good teamwork. Therefore, teamwork is a must for you to fully harness the potential of every member of your network.

- **Greater Flexibility for the Organization**

The conscious effort made to bring employees with different specialization together to work as a team will increase the flexibility of the team. Challenges faced by your business will be easier to solve. Two heads are better than one. Many heads are better than even two heads within certain limits. Mixing people with different but similar skills together in a team will facilitate the sharing of ideas and different perspectives to fix any knot that might impede the progress of your business.

- **Fosters Creativity and Innovation**

One of the major thing teamwork does is that it gives room for all employee to utilize the creativity they've got effectively. Most companies are built around teamwork. Referred to as the flat lattice teamwork-based corporate structure, companies hope to stimulate the best out of their employees by creating a "we" feeling rather than the "I" feeling that traditional business models followed. If you plan to create a self-sustaining business, you need to subscribe to teamwork and its clear advantages.

Understanding Your Team

It is not enough to just set up your talent pool and strengths as an organization in a team; you must be the overall team leader. As the leader, besides contributing to the team, you must also endeavor to understand the team itself. You must understand the way your team works, what spurs them on, and the individual attributes that drives each member of the team. That way, you will know when your team is about to get stumped or when they are on the way to breakthrough.

Teams also work better under different conditions. Many authors and business leaders campaign for their system to be applied to all businesses, but I will tell you today. There is no single way to the ocean. Your team is made up of unique individuals with different skills, attributes, and ideas about work. You need to experiment a bit before you understand what makes your team tick. You need to know what arouses the interest of your team members, and what brings the best in them to the fore.

Some teams work better when they are in a relaxed atmosphere where members can reach into the deepest recesses of their minds to form ideas and conclusions.

An example is the mood Steve Jobs introduced into *Apple* when he took over. His reasoning was that traditional work ethics, such as formal dressing stifled creativity.

He encouraged employees to be at ease in the hope that it would bring their creative best to the fore. Looking at that from here, it looks like a brilliant stroke. *Apple* has continued to wat stronger on this foundation even with Jobs no longer around.

In contrast, we can look at the team that built the hydrogen bombs that ended the Second World War.

The development of the idea had been a long time coming, but progress had been slow until war made it a necessity. Even accounting for increased budgets for weapons research and design, the edgy feeling that ran across that team got the bomb ready in record time.

What I am saying, in essence, is that your team is a unique entity that you need to key into. You need to be able to feel the pulse and rhythm of the team better than anybody else on the team.

You must know when to raise the tempo in the room, and when to defray tempers with a bit of humor. In a way, you are the thermostat for the entire system. You control the way the team works. So, you must understand the team best. Having a clear understanding of the unique strengths that your team has is the best way to ensure your company has all it requires to engage and motivate employees and pave the way for future success.

Here are a few pointers to help you understand

the team better.

• Ask Questions

We have talked about the importance of questions before, but its importance cannot be overstated. Questions allow you as a leader to know the way forward in your desire to leverage the strengths of your employees. Always be on ground to seek clarifications for drop in performance and take insight from individual members. That way, you can be sure every member of the team is on the same page.

• Assess the strength of each member before adding them to the team.

Your business, depending on size, may have more than one team. To this end, you may need to add employees to different teams. Do not just add blindly. Add members to new teams based on their passion, previous ideas, and temperaments. Consider all attributes before throwing a new member into the deep end.

Continuous assessment has to be a key watchword for you. The team needs to identify its unique strength and talent before it can function optimally. To this end, you need to know what you want to achieve with the team and set clear aims and rules of engagement. Do not waste the talent of team members by assigning them to roles they are not suited to.

• Teach the Team to Acknowledge Individual Strengths

A proper understanding of the team is not only meant for you as the overall leader; an avenue should be created for the employees also to assess one another. Every team will have different profiles. There is going to be the optimist who always tries to push the team forward almost carelessly.

There is the cautious individual who considers the repercussions and reactions each decision is likely to evoke.

There is the master planner who can keep everyone on schedule.

There is the creative guru and so on.

Your team is not there to engage one another in frivolous and unhealthy competition. Ensure that the strength of each team-member is factored in, and acknowledged by the whole team. It doesn't mean someone else cannot do their work; it just means they do it best at that moment and need encouragement to keep things burning brightly.

- **Hold A Team Member Story Day**

Yes, take things to a personal level if you want to maximize productivity in your team. That can allow you disarm defenses and allow creativity and idea-sharing to burst forth. Pick a day or two for teammates to tell stories about their experience so far in the establishment and about life in general.

Ensure they include key events, milestones, defining moment, struggles, and other accomplishments. Make it as informal as possible and allow humor to drive home points. You can even go first to warm things up. Keep stories short, about 10 minutes, so that the audience does not get bored, and ask them to include the morals they have acquired from their stories.

Why do you think big companies organize retreats?

Under the guise of learning, retreats allow each member to strip down their professional defenses and interact better with other members of the team outside the working environment.

That alone can subconsciously lift the mood in your camp and keep your team happy and active.

You are only as strong as your team; you must understand and lead your team from the front.

CHAPTER TEN

PRIORITISING VALUE OVER MONEY

"The only competitive advantage in business in any business is one word only, which is "people."

– Kamil Toume

Sadly, most young businesses make a huge mistake; a mistake that plagues them for the rest of our lives. As an entrepreneur, you will be confronted with two choices.

The first choice is the craze to make a profit while the second choice is the need to build a strong pedigree. The mistake most businesses make is that they sacrifice everything for the sake of profit. These companies compromise the quality of their products and services at the expense of profit. While that may be rewarding in the short-term, it is destructive in the long run.

Does this mean that businesses should not be profit-driven? Not at all. A business shouldn't stop looking for ways to make more money; instead, businesses should strike a healthy balance between value delivery and profit-making. Brands that have a name that precedes them are those who have consistently delivered quality products and top-notch services. This is what gives these top brands the pedigree that only a handful of businesses can boast about.

Even though new changes get introduced into the business world every day, old habits refuse to die, and many of them are still circulating in our business world. Technically these bad ideas are serving as a hindrance for so many businesses in this present day. Now is time for you to sit down as a business leader.

Think about where you place your business focus, and assess if you have your head in the right place. Is your business chasing after value or revenues? Is your pedigree rising along with revenues, or are you just focused on generating profit?

The bitter truth is that any company that

prioritizes profit over the creation of value cannot have a say for too long in our present economy. Even with aggressive marketing, your focus will always get known after some time. If your company is *profit-centric,* your clients will get the message and switch to a rival. This is because consumers believe you are there because they are around for you. If they get a hint that you are after your interests rather than their own needs, they will switch focus faster than you can say "Jack Robinson."

Make your company *consumer-centric.* Create value, establish a reputation for catering for your consumers and make your clients the kings they are, and profits will follow. In the business world, your reputation is the best predictor of your future prospects.

I know profit is the ultimate goal of every business, but it should not be your sole motivation. If it is, it will push you into oblivion one way or the other. You should operate your business in such a way that it creates value, not only for the extraction of profit.

When you create value, people will patronize you, and profit will follow. Lamborghinis are highly expensive, but the company has never lacked customers because their product creates a value that other cheaper alternatives cannot. They can even afford to limit the total units of a particular model they want to sell.

Once you become the go-to outlet for value, consumers will troop in and bring the profit you desire. Focus on profit generation at the detriment of value, and your sales will go on the wane sooner rather than later.

Basics on Value Creation and Revenue Extraction

When talking about customer interaction, two significant things are involved, the creation of value, and the extraction of revenue. Definitely, you must have experienced these two concepts in action before, but the idea is that you cannot tell which category you mainly belong. So, to solve this conundrum, let's analyze the attributes of the two concepts.

A business that places focus on value is sure to place customer satisfaction above every other thing, even revenue. Without mincing words, when you create value, your businesses worth increases. This happens in a very practical sense. Customers are more interested in a company that has all it takes to offer them something tangible. When consumers feel like they are getting a product that suits their need or a service that is tailormade for them, they can pay even above the odds.

On the other hand, so many companies still have the firm belief that revenue extraction concept is the most suitable for long-term business.

Now the question is, what is revenue extraction? It's merely a system of operation with the sole aim of making maximum profit. It focuses so much on profit that the idea is to cut down operating costs at all cost. It is the direct opposite of the creation of value. While the creation of value places its focus on serving the customers, revenue extraction is particular about being served its target revenue. Unfortunately, it is a pennywise, pound-foolish business model.

The basic fact is that the type of business operated will show a difference in the response and interaction that will be given to the customers. Although every business needs to place its focus on profit-making to some reasonable extent because any company that's not making a profit will soon close down, you cannot get lost in that cause alone. In the end, clients will ask themselves if they are being served or serve your own commercial needs.

Between 2000 and 2014, Steve Ballmer acted as the CEO of *Microsoft*. Ballmer's focus during this period has been described severally as being on sales and revenue. This attitude contributed mostly to the poor performance of Microsoft in certain years while he was the CEO. Many *Microsoft* products met with unexpected failure and failed to break projections as consumers seemed to reject many offerings from the company.

Unfortunately for the company, *Apple,* its major rival, was doing the direct opposite. That led to a loss of market share for *Microsoft* which the company is still trying to recoup today.

To wrap this up, for you to have the ability and capability to provide the kind of value needed by your customer, you need to consider some important business changes. Precisely, you need to have a clear understanding of what your customers want and make original provisions.

Getting to know what your customers need is essential. If you realize that you have fallen into the category of businesses who think only about profit-making, now is the time for you to start your customer engagement strategy.

You have a chance to create value and make a

profit, why focus on profit alone when you can eat your cake and have it?

CHAPTER ELEVEN

THE BEST BUSINESS VIRTUES TO INCULCATE IN YOUR TEAM

"Ethical living is the indispensable condition of all that is most worthwhile in the world."

— Ernest Caldecott

Virtues cannot be narrowed down to only personal growth, and it is very much applicable to the business world as well.

The virtues of a business can be referred to as those policies and practices embedded in the operation of the company that gives it a positive outlook. The proper understanding of what those policies are is a major component when it comes to ensuring sustainable growth and development in a business

Identification of Top Virtues

On a general note, virtues vary; they depend on the type of company you are running. Having said this, some virtues can be generalized for any business set up. These are the traits that you must allow to shine through your business at all times. They include.

- **Professionalism**

Being professional showcases your competence, expertise, and courtesy in maintaining a better relationship with everyone you come in contact with. Every single action has to be professional to the core. Respect confidentiality and moral obligations that your contract with clients bring even if you do not have a signed agreement to that effect.

- **Versatility**

After you must have come up with ideas, how versatile and flexible you are while staying within a narrow locus will determine how well you maneuver and position your business for success. If you are a genuinely versatile leader, you will be able to remain operational, strategic, compelling, and enabling at all times. Be ready to step into any gap that may occur within your set-up till you craft out a more permanent solution.

• Perseverance

This gives you the strength to survive in the harsh and competitive business climate; every business set up is sure to face challenges. Setting up a business is undoubtedly a game of attrition; it's about you having the discipline and determination to activate your vision. It is of high importance that you do not call it quits when the going gets tough as it will. Instead, make it a habit to persist and dig in. By all means, assess your position from time to time, and do not be too rigid to know when you are wrong. However, do not quit because things get hard. You need to remain consistent and firm in your stand if you ever wish to inspire a group of employees to key into your vision.

• Sustainability

This operates with your initiative, discretion, and your ability to minimize the cost of operation. It's an approach used in the creation of long-term value by giving due consideration to the social, economic, and financial implications of your mode of operation and business system. The core virtue of sustainability is built on the fact that you need to ensure the longevity of your business life. Be careful enough to ensure you do not max out too fast or commit your resources beyond a threshold you cannot operate at.

• Ethical standards

This is all-encompassing as it covers all other virtues. Whatever you do or try, stay on the side of the law. Do not cut corners or you will teach your employees to drive your business into a standstill. Do not give your business a "make-it-at-all-costs" approach that is sure to wreck it for you in no time. Stay vigilant too and regulate all dealings with the public, host communities, clients, and other business associates including rivals. Scandals bury companies faster than they ae built. Stay scandal-free by maintaining the highest form of ethical standards possible.

Why should you imbibe these virtues?

The major reason why the above-listed virtues should be a part of you is to ensure the smooth running of your outfit, even in your absence. Irrespective of the product or service you are providing, you must prioritize the top virtues, and extend them over every aspect of your business. This ranges from your approach towards your employees, your policies, and the procedural effect you choose towards carrying out your business activity. The business virtues are always at the top and represent your business's identity. The virtues you demonstrate will influence the reputation you build with clients and even rival outfits in your niche. It is going to serve as the basis upon which people will relate with your business. It will determine if people come to you with open hands or clenched fists.

After you must have personalized these virtues, you need to make it go viral in your teams. Your business and employees must adopt these core virtues too. It is of utmost importance for them to manifest in your employees. The effort you are meant to make towards this should also be exclusively discussed in the staff meetings. Ensure you reiterate how important your virtues are, and more importantly, how the employees can emulate and showcase these values in dealing with everybody they meet in the process of working for you. It is a primary role for you as the leader to learn new things and impart it upon your team, and business virtues are no exception.

CONCLUSION

What comes to your mind when you picture *Apple* and Steve Jobs together?

The former certainly looks like the personality of the latter.

Picture Bill Gates and *Microsoft,* and it almost seems his laidback attitude is reflected in the easy-to-use operating systems that his company sells.

Elon Musk and his companies sound a lot like "revolutionary." The logo of "The Virgin Group" evokes "great entrepreneurship" in the mind in what seems like the image of the founder, Sir Richard Branson.

A picture of Mark Zuckerberg certainly evokes a feeling of easy networking and causal friendships as espoused by *Facebook.*

These examples should tell you something. The brand goes with the business owner. To succeed in business, you need to build your own team and make it take on your personality. You need to get out there on the frontline and be the foremost ambassador for your business. The image you project for the public gets associated with your company. Therefore, you must work on your personality. There is no other choice.

A great business is built on unique products or service delivery and creating value. To do this, you need a vibrant team where members dovetail nicely to give you the edge you need to make an impact in your niche.

Most importantly though, your team needs you to be a proactive, warm and efficient team-leader. You do not even need to be better than your employees in execution of tasks. Steve Jobs wasn't the best tech mind at Apple, Andrew Carnegie paid the first million-dollar wage in history to Charles Schwab to manage men more knowledgeable than himself to run his steel mills.

What you must do though is to get involved in making sure your teamwork functions efficiently and in line with your vision.

In the end, you are your business, and your business is you. Nobody can lead your team into battle better than you. Be the leader your team needs. Make your business your concern and begin to lead it onto success today!